PEOPLE, PLACES, & QUILTS

PEOPLE, PLACES, & QUILTS

DIANE F. WILSON

EPM
PUBLICATIONS, INC.

Library of Congress Cataloging-in-Publication Data

Wilson, Diane.
People, places & quilts: from vibrant pieces of cloth and memory, a contemporary folk artist limns her family's odyssey with the U.S. Navy / Diane Wilson.
    p.   cm.
 ISBN 0-939009-30-7
  1. Wilson, Diane. 2. Quiltmakers—United States—Biography. 3. Wilson, Diane—Family. I. Title. II. Title: People, places, and quilts.
NK9198.W55A2   1989
746.9′7′092—dc20
[B]   89-39906
                                                CIP

Copyright © 1989 Diane Wilson
All rights reserved
EPM Publications, Inc., 1003 Turkey Run Road,
  McLean, Virginia 22101
Printed in the United States of America

Cover and book design by Tom Huestis

CONTENTS

Introduction 9

1.
1963–65 *Idaho, Connecticut, California, Washington* 10

2.
1965–69 *Virginia, South Carolina, Connecticut* 15

3.
1969–72 *Hawaii, South Carolina* 25

4.
1972–75 *Connecticut* 31

5.
1975–78 *South Carolina* 37

6.
1978–81 *Scotland* 47

7.
1981–85 *South Carolina, Virginia* 57

8.
1985– *Virginia* 69

Epilogue 85

Thoughts 88

DRAWING CREDITS

CHRIS CONNELL, *Holy Trinity Church*
RON SCARBOUGH, *Pace Print Preview*

COLOR PHOTO CREDITS

MICHAEL LATIL, *All color photos with the following exceptions*

JOHN GARETTI/BETTER HOMES AND GARDENS, *Amish Quilt, Lady Bugs, Rainbow Farm.*

MAJE WALDO, *"Moon Over the Mountain".*

BLACK AND WHITE PHOTO CREDITS

ELEANOR BROWNLEE KOETS, Front Porch, Train Coming up From Lincolnville, Edesto Photos, Wesa, Tennis Player, St. Paul's Church, Citadel Cadet, Looking for Sharks' Teeth (Porch Rocker Recollections), *Grown Up Babies, Priscilla Button, Alden & Elizabeth, Sammy.*

BEE CEE KUPERSMITH, Wilson Family.

LEDGER-STAR, Meadowbrook Students and Me.

PAM MINOR, Diane F. Wilson.

HOWARD PARK, John and Rooie

PAT TRIMM, Julia, Wilson Children

JAMES RUSSELL WILSON, Okra, Turtle, Annie Carter, Bucket, Woody's Pond, Patterns, Books, Tennis Magazine Letter, "Summerville Scene", Dr. Lewis's Page, Letter/Poem, "Holy Loch", Children, USNA Graduates, Company Sign, Compulsive Jacket Sketch, "Go Skins" Sketch, 206 E. Richardson Ave.

A special thanks to the following people who made this book possible

KAREN AKIN, JUDY ANDERSON, BARBARA BAILEY, CONNIE BENSE, DUNCAN BLAIR, SUSAN BLAIR, SOLVEIG BROWNFELD, PRISCILLA BUTTON, BARBARA CANDLER, MARIA CARLUZZO, BERNARD CHAPEL, VICKY DAVIS, SUZANNE DVELLS, CATHY EASLEY, NORBERT FRANKENBERGER, SUZANNE FRANKENBERGER, SAMMY GAILLARD, TOMMIE GERLINGER, W. CAPEHART HARVEY, MARTHA HAYNES, AUDREY HEARD, ELIZABETH HILT, RICHARD HILT, DAVID ISABEL, HELEN ISABEL, DIXIE KAUFMAN, DON KOETS, ELEANOR KOETS, JOSEPH KOETS, JULIA KOETS, THOMAS KVAN, PEGGY KWIST, MICHAEL LATIL, COL. BEN LEGARE, SANDRA LESOURD, ELSPETH LEWIS, NADINE LOMAX, ELAINE MANNEN, ELIZABETH MEYERS, PAM MINOR, LAURIE MYERS, JANE MITCHELL, NANCY MOSELEY, BOB PENN, PEGGY PENN, ANNE SANDLUND, CHRIS SENSENEY, ELSPETH SHAW, MARTIN SHAW, MADELINE SHEPPERSON, KATIE STOLZFUS, SARA TEMPLETON, BETSY THOMPSON, EDEN THROWER, TAY VIERRA, WESA WARING, ALDEN WERSTLER, GINGA WILDER, JAMES WILSON, JERUSHA WILSON, JIM WILSON, JOHN WILSON, JULIA WILSON

To the publisher and editor,
EVELYN METZGER,
and to designer, TOM HUESTIS—
also a special thanks!

Dedicated to
JEANNE MITCHLER-FIKS
who knew I could,
and POOKA GLIDDEN *and* MARLA REISCH
who showed me how.

Jim and Diane cutting the wedding cake. Mare Island, California, 1963.

There we were, smiling and looking apprehensive. Jim was a Lt. j.g. in the Navy and I was Mrs. James R. Wilson.

Introduction

This book tells a story. About people, places and quilts. I've moved more times than I care to count. Met some wonderful people, some that weren't, and made quilts through it all. Twenty-five years worth.

Growing up, I never thought of making a quilt. Sewing brought nothing but frustration. I did love drawing and painting. Then, I happened to see a picture of a quilt in *Time* magazine. It sounds dramatic, but this is true: something stirred inside me. That was how it started.

Quilting provided an outlet for me ... for creativity—I like to make things with my hands, and to vent frustration. I longed to spend my life with someone who was never really there. Making quilts set things right.

These quilts aren't *the best*. There are quilts with finer stitches, more elaborate patterns. But, these *are* special quilts. It's all in the story.

A page from *Time* magazine.

This was the beginning for me. I saw this quilt and loved it. Colors, design, everything.

1963–65
Idaho, Connecticut, Washington

I was born into a military family and so were my parents—no roots. While living in California I met and married a naval officer (swore I never would). I was just nineteen and thought I knew it all.

I remember California to this day—brown hills that turned green over-

10

night once the rains came, the clean smell of eucalyptus trees, driving along the Old Coast Road, the fog and those fields full of flowers owned by the seed companies, the small towns John Steinbeck wrote about. What a place! No wonder people went west.

After getting married, we moved to Idaho. I remember silver dollars for change, cold and snow, no money, cowboy boots and Admiral Hyman Rickover. I feel the same way about him as I do Ann Landers. So much common sense.

After Idaho we moved to Connecticut and that is where John was born. We were there about six months, then headed back to California. On the way across country we stopped in Illinois to visit with my husband Jim's relatives.

Aunt Dees gave us a quilt as a late wedding present. It was lovely, soft with age and use, and not what I wanted. I liked really bright colors and these were pastel.

I started my first quilt in California. We were living in Coronado, before the bridge was built. I was twenty years old, John was just a baby and I washed his white shoelaces every night because everything had to be perfect. I was sure Dr. Spock left out whole chapters of his book. I really didn't know what to do with this baby. It was a lonely time. I did meet other young moms. But, instead of getting support from each other, we left the walks and beach feeling inadequate. It was the recitals of who was sitting up, crawling, walking, potty trained, the stress. I had no idea it was just the start.

We moved to Bremerton, Washington—beautiful with lots of rain. We lived next door to a Puget Power substation. Our small basement apartment had ugly linoleum floors and, worse, I remember a babysitter stole my jewelry and twenty dollars hidden in a top drawer.

After a couple of months we moved back to California and I finally finished the quilt. Whenever I'm short of money, I think of that twenty dollars.

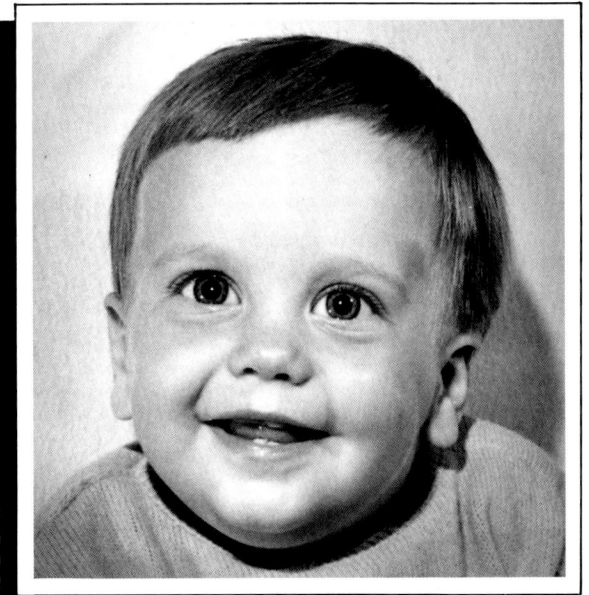

John Chase Wilson. About nine months old. Coronado, California, 1965.

This business of everybody's first name starting with a "J" is not my doing. I would have preferred an Emily or Henry. I did get to pick the middle names.

Four Patch. 1965.
82″ × 66″. Cotton.
Diane F. Wilson.

My first quilt. I would have liked to have made the quilt in the picture, but I hadn't the faintest idea where to start. My landlady who knew everything said, "A quilt is simple to make. Just sew some squares together and that will be the top. And then something goes in the middle. And then there is the bottom, of course."

There is a pattern of sorts. I remember taking care to match the prints with the solids. Most of the squares were from dresses and curtains—I loved this quilt. Still do. It is faded and worn out. The batting is all lumpy in places, and some squares are mended with stitching just to hold the batting in. I feel like this quilt.

Dresden Plate Quilt. Circa 1935. 92" × 74". Cotton. Louise Wilson McClusky (Aunt Dees).

Aunt Dees gave us this quilt. I didn't like it at first. Too pale. Sort of like living in Marion. Small town or used to be. The men drove and talked about big cars. The women all had tight gray curls, like halos all around their heads. After supper— navy beans, sliced onions, and fresh tomatoes—off we'd go . . . driving!

  Past cornfields . . . "doing good."
  Past cemeteries . . . "folks buried there."
  Past coal mines . . . "closed down now."
  And in later years, past the new penitentiary . . . "ever see anything like that?"
  BORING! It took a while, but I came to appreciate this quilt and life in a small town. I wanted the security, the slow and gentle way of life that allows people to sit in those funny metal chairs under trees and to talk. About everything and nothing.

Annie Carter with Jerusha. Alvin, South Carolina. 1968.

"Well look here. Did you ever see such a thing?"

I looked but only saw a baby sleeping.

"Her ears, see how they lay right up along side her head? Jest like little shells."

2.
1965–69
Virginia, South Carolina, Connecticut

I started my second quilt in Virginia. We had left California, headed across country, stopping in Illinois of course, and now were living for a few months in Virginia Beach. Without having any idea of how to applique, I started in. So frustrating!

We moved down to South Carolina at the end of six months. My first time ever in the Deep South. We lived in a terrible neighborhood in Goose Creek. Whenever someone moved out, the neighbors all went over and dug up the shrubbery.

Well, I had put the applique quilt aside and made two patchwork quilts on the sewing machine for John's bunk beds. Awful lumpy things of red, white, and blue squares. I was in a hurry, plain and simple, and made a mess. It seems I was always in a hurry to get things straight and settled. We moved so often that I felt if we weren't settled in a week, we never would be.

Our neighbors were an older couple, Annie and Zeb Carter. Wonderful people. I couldn't have lasted in that neighborhood five minutes without them. Both helped me get going again on the applique quilt, gave advice, encouragement and taught me how to garden.

Annie and Zeb moved to their own farm in Alvin, and we moved to a small town Jim had heard about from friends at work, Summerville. We bought our first house there. A cottage with a tin roof, front porch, big windows with ripply glass and a real clothes line out back. To "fit in" you only had to attend church on Sunday and the football games Friday nights.

Our new neighbor was Mrs. Westmoreland. Her dad had built our house. Over the years Mrs. W. became our best friend. We borrowed everything she owned. She knew everybody and everything and told us all she knew. After

Front Porch

I think front porches are wonderful. Front steps are nice too. I have sat on this porch and rocked babies, called dogs off guests, smelled the aroma from the logging trucks as they roared past (hey, speed limit's 25 here!) and worked on quilts. There is a tea olive bush to one side, and the smell puts me in the nicest place.

church on Sunday we would take Mrs. Westmoreland for strawberry pie at Shoney's over on Route 52.

Jerusha was born while we were living in Summerville. It was late one night. Jim and I had just finished canning some pickles when I knew it was time. We quick called Mrs. W., who rushed right over. She was always there for us.

I continued to work on my quilt. But I had to "eat my spinach before I could have my cake." The house had to be cleaned, the clothes hung out, the yard

Myrtle Hendley Westmoreland, about 1968.

Mrs. Westmoreland hated to have her picture taken. She's standing here in back of the boat shed. The old wash tub hanging up was used for bathing her dog, George, a poodle. I never cared for poodles until I met George. The fence was hidden in the summer by tall yellow flowers. Mrs. W. used the roots to make Jerusalem artichoke relish and pickles. I never cared for either. Tasted like dirt. I loved Mrs. Westmoreland.

"I don't have any aggravations as of late, at least not since Bill died."

"I'll tell it to you true, Martha Claire didn't learn a thing in college, except how to smoke."

17

Jerusha Suzanne Wilson, about 18 months. 1969.

Rooie (Jerusha's nickname) is wearing a dress Aunt Dees made for her. I wanted to name her Suzanne Louise. Suzanne for my mom, and Louise for Jim's mom and aunt. But this "J" business got in the way.

After all these years, I'm still not sure about this name. We saw it the other night, though. I was reading a book to James and Julia and there it was!

"Oh, my! but ain't she handsome!

Dear me! She's the sweetest name!

Ky! Yi! to love her is my dooty,

My pretty, little, posy-pink

Jenny Jerusha Jane"**

The First Four Years *by Laura Ingalls Wilder.*

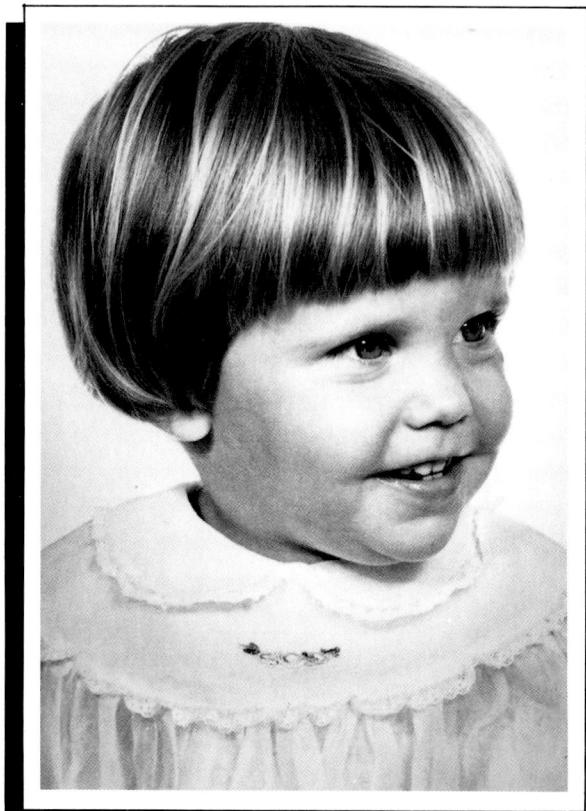

raked, pets fed, kids "straight," dinner fixed. Then, I would let myself do something that I liked. The only trouble was, I was too worn out.

We were in Summerville only a year before we moved again, back to Connecticut. We returned all of Mrs. Westmoreland's things, rented our house, and headed north. Jim had found a house for us out in the country by a pond.

We loved it there. Wildflowers and cows in the fields, snakes, turtles, ducks, swans, and muskrats around and in the pond—it was lovely and lonely. We knew only one person, Woody. He owned all the property around the house and knew where all the birds' nests were.

After just eight months we left Woody, unhatched turtle eggs, and Connecticut and started on our way to Hawaii. John, Rooie and I were to fly across country, stopping on the way to visit relatives. Jim was to ride a submarine around.

We were staying with Aunt Dees when I finished all the quilt squares. We had the quilt together and the quilting started when I left Dees and Illinois for my parent's home in California. Dees put us on the plane, told the kids "to be good," and told me "to always vote the straight Republican ticket and keep up the quilting."

Okra

What does it taste like?
"Real good. Why, there is nothing better. Just fry it up along side yer meat."

Woody's Pond. Old Mystic, Connecticut. 1969. Diane F. Wilson.

To the west past Old Mystic on Route 184, and just to the left, is a pond. High's Pond. But I renamed it Woody's Pond. Woody had been named for Woodrow Wilson, and he told me his mother received a letter from the president himself commenting on the fact. Woody had a tractor that he used to mow the fields with. He named it Mr. John and showed us where all the birds' nests were.

Bucket

Woody gave me this bucket out of his barn at the top of our road. The barn was filled with junk that Woody picked out of the Stonington town dump.
"Some fool used it for clamming. See, they punched holes in the bottom, but you could still use it for something."
I used to spend hours polishing this bucket, a routine. Not anymore. Now, it's not so important to have things shine.

Turtle

Once hanging out clothes, I heard a rustling in the leaves. It was a turtle! There's something nice about having a turtle in your yard.

The Allen Hovey Wilson family of Williamson County, Illinois. 1915.

"It was an Indian summer day. Late October. We were all there for the fiftieth anniversary of my grandparents. Allen and Mary Wilson. I can tell you everybody's name this minute. Remember them all. I was real sick that day. Threw up over to the side there right before the photographer took the picture."

Dees is in the second row, third from the right.

20

Lowell, Russell, and Jack Wilson. Hurst, Illinois. 1930's.

All killed in the war. Such a loss would seem overwhelming.

"Oh, that fellow was a hot shot all right. Flew a desk during the War. Not like our boys."

"Dad was furious when he heard about him getting his son out of serving. Sent him a yellow shirt. We like to have died. Dad said he didn't do it. But, I know he did."

Hosea and Eula Wilson, their six children, and Grandma Wilson (Mary). Hurst, Illinois. 1929.

Dees, Grandma Wilson, Jack, Russell, Lowell, Eula, Kathryn, Hosea and Ronald.

Hosea was a school teacher, principal, and, in time, superintendent of schools for Hurst/Bush, Illinois. Eula was the daughter of Lippidorus Hannibal Russell (what a name). Dees taught for awhile, then worked for the Ben and Zoller Coal Company. Kathryn married. All the boys went into the military. All were killed in World War II except Ronald. His ship was hit by a kamikazi and sunk in 49 seconds. He survived.

Dresden Plate Quilt. Circa 1935. 92" × 55". Cotton. Louise Wilson McClusky.

Aunt Dees made "about" 15 quilts. I have three, two like this and the purple one. I think all of Dees' quilts were pieced and made between 1931 and 1946.

"I would just sit and listen to the radio, after work, war news and all, piecing the latest quilt. I got the patterns from neighbors and we got the fabric from a dress factory over in Herrin. Mother and a neighbor helped with the quilting."

Dees' kitchen was all pink—refrigerator, stove, freezer, table, chairs, floor, walls, cabinets—everything except the curtains. They were white with flowers, along the bottom. Dees would sit at her pink table, smoking a cigarette with each cup of coffee, spreading whipped butter on dry toast.

"I feel weak as a cat. Haven't got a speck of energy for doing much of anything."

"Maybe you should quit smoking, Dees."

"Hell, I'd rather die from smoking than from a'wanting to!"

Applique Album Quilt. 1967.
90" × 75". Cotton.
Diane F. Wilson.

My second quilt. (Fourth, really, if I count the two awful patchwork quilts I made for John's bunk beds.) Annie and Zeb Carter helped me with this quilt, which was to be like the one in Time *magazine. Annie said, "jest get some squares, enough to cover the bed, and make a picture in each one." Zeb said, "you got to turn the edges under."*

The first square, the one on the top left corner is awful. I didn't know how to applique, that's for sure. But I got better. I copied some designs from the picture then just started making them up as I went and we moved. Mrs. Westmoreland's daffodils are there, poppies for California, and chicory—I love its blue flowers all along the highways—and those are strips from an old blouse my mom made.

I was staying with Aunt Dees when I finally finished all those squares. Dees showed me how to measure evenly, hide knots, applique and how to quilt. Dees came right out and said that first square was not so hot, and she suggested we leave it out, that she would help me do another quick. I said no, I wanted it left in to remind me of what it was to start and get better.

I finished the quilt in California, put those points around the border like Dees had suggested. The quilt had taken almost three years to make. I thought it was beautiful.

**Hawaiian Quilt.
Orchid. 1970.**
90″ × 90″. Cotton.
Diane F. Wilson.

The hardest quilt I have ever made. Twenty-seven yards of fabric. Nine each for top, applique and bottom. (It was expensive back in those days to buy that much fabric.) Seems like a lot, but you needed every bit. Picture this. You take nine yards and cut it into three yard sections. Then, sew it back together the "fat" way to make a three yard square. The part to be cut was folded a certain way. Can't tell it all here now, but a bit like making a snowflake.

Usually, according to "tutu" (Hawaiian for grandmother or teacher), these quilts are done in solid colors and quilted like this—reiterating the applique design. Like Pacific Ocean waves.

I didn't like these quilts at all at first. They seemed too bright, too bold. Almost tacky. Like paintings on velvet.

Of all my quilts, this has won the most ribbons, the most praise. Except once a fat man told me at a show in Connecticut, "The quilting's awful. I could catch my big toe in it!" Ha! I thought. No way would that ever happen because your fat toe would never be near it! My stitches did get smaller.

3.

1969–72
Hawaii, South Carolina

I had dreamed of living in a tropical paradise. Especially on cold rainy days. But it wasn't so easy for a lot of reasons. The expense for one thing. Rents and houses were sky high! And the prejudice.

Anyone who was not a "local" was really discriminated against. Everywhere we went. Of course, this was a good lesson for us. It's maddening to be disliked or feared because of something you can't help or change. Not like being a jerk. A person can change that!

Another type of prejudice was just as bad. This one was against the military and anyone connected with the military. It was during the height of the Viet Nam War and there were some hostile feelings, I can tell you, and the feelings weren't against the "enemy."

I felt this hostility at every turn. It felt awful. I wanted my lonely months alone to count for a good cause, not an evil one. War is awful. I sure don't have the answer. Maybe using words to disarm. Honesty, trust, ... a big order when most of the world is dysfunctional. (Mental health starts at home. Ha!)

Then, the other wives. Ugh. Like the young moms in California, we could have been such a support to each other. We weren't. The talk had passed beyond babies. Now it was who was taking what lessons, attending which school, promoted early to what rank, invited to whose party. Blah! I seemed to be the only one who had a hard time coping with a husband who was home three months, gone three and a half, home three, gone, etc.

It wasn't all bad of course. Nothing ever is. I learned to make Hawaiian quilts and met Ellen. She helped me start to learn that the world wouldn't fall apart if I relaxed my watch on children, weeds and dust.

Needlepoint Rug. 1973.

6′ × 3′. Wool. Diane F. Wilson.

After three years, I finished the Hawaiian quilt, had my picture taken with it even, in color, for the Charleston paper. That was that, I thought, the end of quilts. I started in on a needlepoint rug. I made it to match the Hawaiian quilt, that's why the colors are wild.

  Well, it turned into one frustrating mess. The pen I used to mark the design said "indelible." It was a red pen and the darned thing bled all over everything when the rug was blocked.

  I wonder how those people who make those guarantees can sleep nights.

Hawaiian Quilt Patterns.

Tutu said the designs or patterns were made from the shadows cast by a plant or animal. (I tried this once and it worked.) The patterns are bold and modern looking, I think.

  Tutu said the patterns were a closely guarded secret and never shared. She said that when quilts were washed they were hung to dry inside out so neighbors couldn't copy them.

  Tutu guarded her patterns also. She kept them all mashed between the pages of a Sears and Roebuck catalogue.

When it was time to move, I had no regrets. We were moving back to Summerville.

Mrs. Westmoreland was glad to have us back. We fell right in where we left off. We didn't have to drive over to Route 52 for strawberry pie. There was a Shoney's in town now, and a Hardees.

I joined a tennis group, met more people, and was just glad to be back in my own house again. My only worry was all the social obligations that went with Jim's advance in rank. I had no training for my job. I felt uncomfortable. I grew to resent the lost time and energy spent on these military obligations.

The Hawaiian quilt was finally finished. I started on a needlepoint rug, and it was time to move again. Jim had orders back to Connecticut. We cleaned up the house, painted it inside and out. I hated to leave it for someone else to enjoy.

Train coming up from Lincolnville.

We could hear this train coming about two minutes before it reached Summerville. The tracks are only one block from our house. The children and I would shout to each other, "Train's coming!," then we would run like crazy down to the tracks arriving just in time to see the engine light grow big before our eyes.

I love trains . . . the power, the motion, the noise, the life they give a town. This one sped right through without stopping, its speed making my very insides vibrate. The size and noise made my children, depending on how old they were, cling tightly to my neck, arms or legs.

Edisto Photos

The same friends that told us about Summerville told us about Edisto Beach. There might be better beaches, but it depends on what you're after.

The ride to Edisto is almost as wonderful as the beach. All back roads, flat to start, lined with mostly pine trees, needles baking in the hot sun. What a smell. Then, open fields with packing sheds by railroad tracks, packed themselves with people, tomatoes, cucumbers.

Next, soft gray shacks with kitchen appliances on the porches, lines with washing blowing in the hot air, churches, scrawny dogs, then the final bends, oak woods, marsh and at last, Edisto.

Dirt Road, Edisto Island.

Edisto Marsh Creek.

These creeks are full of oysters, fish, crabs, shrimp and, sometimes alligators!

The Old Post Office, Edisto Island.

John and Rooie. Mystic, Connecticut. About 1973.

We went on a lot of trips through New England, staying at country inns. I thought it was fun and relaxing to look at the scenery, but from the back seat came, "I'm tired, I'm hungry, I'm thirsty, I have to go to the bathroom, I'm bored, I wanna go home."

25 Pequot Avenue.

Our house in Mystic. There was a terrific garage out back built of stones and wood. It was prettier than the house. Would have made a great studio. Jim found an old bottle of peach brandy hidden in the rafters.

4.
1972–75
Connecticut

We rented a house in Noank, back in the woods, got two kittens, Sally and Susan, one for John and one for Rooie. There was a cemetery behind us and, to the right, our only close neighbor, Mrs. Brown. I got the worst case of poison ivy I've ever had clearing her driveway.

After not quite a year, we bought an old house over in Mystic and moved there. We filled it with old oak furniture. For a while there, if it was oak, we bought it. One day Jim suggested we get rid of this old oak roll top desk I had bought and refinished. I suggested we get rid of an old oak dining room set he had bought and refinished. We went through the whole house before it was over, getting rid of more than furniture. Then we bought old pine, already refinished.

I had the best garden I can remember—corn, asparagus, beets, cucumbers, tomatoes, several kinds of lettuce, squash, zucchini, spinach. I canned until I cried. We had two pear trees also. I canned the fruit making spiced pears and pear chutney. It became a compulsion. To this day, I can hardly eat a pear.

I met two people who were really interested in quilts while living here. Before then, wherever we moved, I had been the only one that seemed to be quilting.

Audrey had a shop that sold quilts and quilted pillows. Sharon taught quilting and was writing a book about how to quilt. Both had lots of experience and confidence. I needed both.

Sharon's book, *The Great Noank Quilt Factory*, is one of my favorites because it is so easy to understand. Several of my things are in there. Audrey decided to write a book because Sharon did.

I never ever again worked at quilting as hard as I did during that one year. I can't believe I made all the things

The Great Noank Quilt Factory by **Sharon McKain.**
The Complete Guide to Quilting by **Audrey Heard and Beverly Pryor.**

Sharon's book is my favorite of the two. Much easier to understand. Both books have my work in them. It was an exciting time. Ideas, deadlines, interviews. Looking back, I don't know how I did it all. My family suffered, I know.

Moon Over the Mountain. 1972.
Wall Hanging. Cotton.
Diane F. Wilson.

The first piece I made and then sold—at a gallery in Newport, Rhode Island. I've always liked African designs. I was on a run at using these particular colors. Sometimes it lasted months—everything would be only certain colors.

I did. I must have been quilting morning, noon and night.

There was a crowd from Noank I ran around with. I was fascinated by their ways—wild and relaxed. A Bohemian bunch I guess. It seemed glamorous at the time. Looking back, I'd have to say it was irresponsible.

Jim worked long hours, never getting home before 9:00 or 10:00 p.m. I just put the kids to bed and sewed. In time, Jim was selected for command of his own submarine and left for school in Washington, D.C.

I remember resenting being left behind, not being asked if I wanted to go (I didn't, but I wanted the choice). Jim bought a new VW "bug," new suits, took the clock radio and off he went.

I liked living in Connecticut, we had lived there twice before. Even now I can remember the crisp clean air and know what each season feels like.

Hawaiian Quilt. *Avocado.* **1973.**
70" × 70". Cotton. Diane F. Wilson.

Sharon and I decided to test the Hawaiian method of making patterns. We traced the shadow Sharon's avocado plant made, and with some artistic license, came up with this design.

Some of the quilts appearing in The Complete Guide to Quilting.

Rainbow Farm. 1973.
Full. Cotton. Diane F. Wilson.

I made this quilt for a lady who has a farm of the same name in Vermont. Originally she wanted it done in pink and blue only.

Amish Diamond. 1973.
90" × 90". Cotton. Diane F. Wilson.

Lady Bug. 1973.
65" × 65". Cotton. Diane F. Wilson.

34

Jim's Quilt. Amish Diamond Variation. 1975.

85" × 60". Cotton. Diane F. Wilson.

Jim received this quilt as a present. He was to be CO (Commanding Officer) of his own submarine now. The USS George Barcroft, SSBN 643 Gold. Can you see all the quilting? The quilting is all of nautical symbols—command-at-sea pin, dolphins, rope, tridents, anchors, a submarine—United States Navy initials and Jim's name.

John's Quilt. 1975.

80" × 60". Cotton. Diane F. Wilson.

McCall's Contemporary Quilting published this back in 1976. I was so proud and excited. Even though I measured and worked it out on graph paper ahead of time— the stripe (with blue triangle) didn't quite meet the edges. However, if it was all right with McCalls, *it was all right with me.*

I made two of these quilts for John's bunk beds. He had been using those awful lumpy ones all this time.

John at this age could outrun me. I remember that. And, that we argued constantly about whether he would wear any kind of coat.

Rooie's Quilt. *House on the Hill*. 1975.

80" × 55". Cotton. Diane F. Wilson.

I have always loved this pattern but will be the first to admit that my piecing is not the best. Several of the houses are made from Rooie's baby dresses. Also, there is a funny spot where the cat, Sally, threw up. The other cat, Susan, went up to the schoolyard each lunchtime and finally just stayed there full-time.

St. Paul's Church. Summerville, South Carolina.

The quilt show was held at the church's parish hall, around back. I'm reminded of a true story . . .

A friend said that they didn't see him in church.

He told them he was in the back.

Oh, they said, they were in the back, too. Well, he said, he was way in the back.

Oh, they were too. In the very back. So where in the back was he?

Way back. Back home!

5.

1975–78
South Carolina

It was hard to leave Connecticut, but we had no choice. Packed up the cat, houseplants, kids, rented the house and headed down 95. Back to Summerville. Always a good place to go back to.

Town had grown even more. Now there was a McDonalds. And the fire whistle didn't blow for volunteers anymore. They were already there. Paid members, sitting out front across from the Coca-Cola bottling plant, watching the trucks come and go.

I "found" religion this time back. No fooling. Just like Jimmy Carter. I joined a bible study group—all different faiths. It was the first time for me. I always was real uncomfortable around people with black bibles, standing on street corners talking about "Jeeeeesus." I thought the bible study group might be the same. It wasn't. I learned that there is more to life than fear and guilt.

We added onto our house and family. James was born just three days after Jim left for three and half months at sea. My parents came to help out. That was a nice time.

Jim was Commanding Officer now and I was expected to look after all the wives. I did my best but the truth was, I needed someone to look after me.

I made quilts, cleaned house, drove kids to piano, basketball and soccer practice, and tried to cope with a small baby, moody nine-year-old and a teenager who resented his dad's absence.

At the end of three and one half years, an incredible time for us to be in one place, let alone one house, Jim had orders to Guam. We were so excited! An island, beaches, shells, surfing! Two weeks before we were to go, Jim's orders were changed. We were going to Scotland.

Wesa

Wesa smoked those brown thin cigarettes, wore hats to control her hair, had long fingernails painted red and called me "darlin." She owned a second-hand store in town that I visited almost everyday, after I picked up the mail at the post office.

Totem Pole. 1977.
106" × 38". Cotton/cotton blends. Diane F. Wilson.

Indians always seemed so romantic, and I liked totem poles so that is how this came to be. A bear is at the top, then a mountain goat, big foot is next (I had just watched a stupid TV movie about him), then a turtle, next an eagle, then a salmon and lastly Wesa, a friend. She asked to be low man on my totem pole. Why not?

Somehow, we got our passports, shots, warm clothes and left from an Air Force Base in New Jersey. But not before we had waited sixteen hours in a small room with crying babies, grumpy tired children, impatient adults and cigarette smokers. For a plane that was to be leaving "any minute."

Suzanne Sullivant Chase and Norbert Frankenberger. April, 1942.

My parents on their wedding day.

Hawaiian Quilt. *Lily of the Valley.* 1978.
90" × 90". Cotton. Diane F. Wilson.

I made this for my parents 35th wedding anniversary. My mom's favorite flower has always been lily of the valley. I think this quilt might look better if the color scheme were reversed.

Flower Bouquet. 1949.

96" × 80". Cotton. Suzanne C. Frankenberger.

My mom made this from a kit she bought while living in Hawaii. The pink along the bottom is a different color from the rest because I cut up the original pink for doll clothes. Mom said she paid someone $25.00 to quilt it for her.

Nancy's Wedding Quilt. 1974.

Double. Cotton. Diane F. Wilson

By the time this quilt was finished, the marriage was too. Back then, I was completely unaware of the pain and sadness each person felt. Selfishly I thought of my feelings only—that my time had been wasted making something special for two people who were no longer together. I had a lot to learn.

Tennis Quilt. *Anyone for . . . . 1978.*

100" × 80". Cotton/cotton blends. Diane F. Wilson.

I enjoyed playing tennis. Met some really nice people. Good exercise and all that. I didn't like to play with Jim though. He took it all so seriously.

This quilt appeared in Tennis *magazine. I gave them the directions too, which was a mistake. I'm terrible at math.*

40

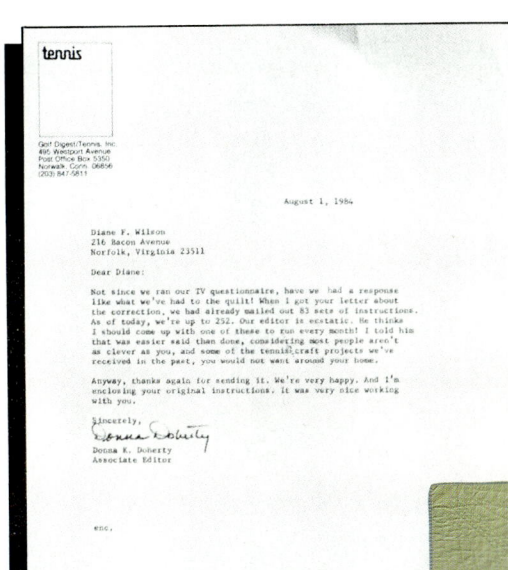

Letter from editor at *Tennis* magazine.

Tennis Player

The women who played tennis at the country club came decked out in some incredible outfits—matching everything, eye shadow, jewelry. Then it occurred to me, this wasn't tennis anymore, this was SEX.

Nadine's Quilt. 1977.
Double. Cotton. Diane F. Wilson.

I consider this one of the best quilts I ever quilted. An easy piecing pattern, but hard quilting pattern. It was to match some designs in Nadine's crewel drapes. It took years for my fingers to make really small stitches. Now, I can still make small stitches. I just can't see them!

Newspaper clipping, "The Summerville Scene." 1979.

Someone sent this to me while we were living in Scotland. Apparently, there was a bigger write-up in Time.

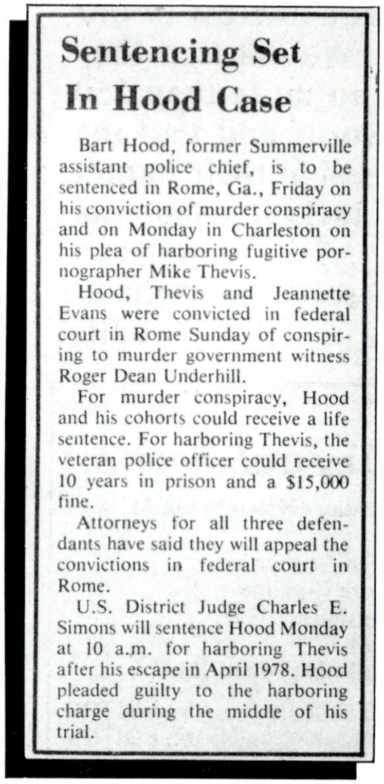

James Norbert Wilson, about nine months.

John and Rooie were so happy to have a little brother. Before he was born, we borrowed a bassinet from friends and fixed it up. I was using a lot of green, I guess, because John asked, "What's this kid gonna be? A Martian or something?"

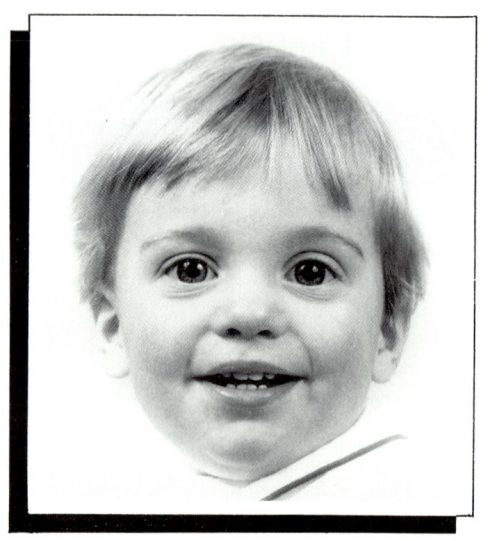

Baby Quilts

All my friends had babies, it seemed. I made quilts for most.

***Croak.* 1978.**
42" × 36". Cotton.
Diane F. Wilson.

James's quilt. It seems everyone of my friends had babies too. It was a happy time.

Sentencing Set In Hood Case

Bart Hood, former Summerville assistant police chief, is to be sentenced in Rome, Ga., Friday on his conviction of murder conspiracy and on Monday in Charleston on his plea of harboring fugitive pornographer Mike Thevis.

Hood, Thevis and Jeannette Evans were convicted in federal court in Rome Sunday of conspiring to murder government witness Roger Dean Underhill.

For murder conspiracy, Hood and his cohorts could receive a life sentence. For harboring Thevis, the veteran police officer could receive 10 years in prison and a $15,000 fine.

Attorneys for all three defendants have said they will appeal the convictions in federal court in Rome.

U.S. District Judge Charles E. Simons will sentence Hood Monday at 10 a.m. for harboring Thevis after his escape in April 1978. Hood pleaded guilty to the harboring charge during the middle of his trial.

Banner. 1978.
96″ × 20″. Cotton.
Diane F. Wilson.

I made this banner to advertise a quilt show we were having at St. Paul's Church to raise money for the local "Y."

People in town had given some beautiful old family quilts for the show, and I was worried about the safety of the quilts. My mom, who was visiting, suggested hiring an off-duty policeman. I did. Bart Hood. He was pencil thin, and he wouldn't take any money for looking after the quilts that one night. Said he was doing it for "the Lord."

North Carolina Lily Variation. 1977.
64″ × 60″. Cotton.
Diane F. Wilson.

I made this for fun. The only weird thing I have ever made. I thought I made it because I loved this pattern but also because I had read a really depressing book, We Have Always Lived in a Castle, *by Shirley Jackson. A story about two sisters who went crazy.*

43

Fish. 1977.
5′ × 3′. Cotton. Diane F. and Rooie Wilson.

There were friends in town who had a New Year's Eve party every year. It meant a lot to get an invitation. Those that didn't were crushed.

One year the theme was your zodiac sign. Rooie and I made this fish in 2 1/2 hours. I wore it. My head came out of his mouth—and the parts on either side were on my shoulders. I hate costume parties. Too much effort to be clever.

A friend remarked, "I don't necessarily want to go to any parties. I just want the invitation." Exactly!

Eden's Quilt. 1978.
Single. Cotton/cotton blends. Diane F. Wilson.

A friend of a friend wanted this quilt made for her husband's son who was going off to school—to Sewanee to be exact. (I had never heard of it, except in a song.)

After the quilt was finished and picked up, I never expected to see it again. But I did. And when I did I was surprised to see that a college student, who was by then young adult, had really cared for this quilt. Though it had been well used, it was in almost perfect condition; had only one stain that came out with Tide and Shout! (I always feel I am part of my quilts; it's important to me that they are cared for.)

45

"The Hollies," Dunoon, Scotland.

Our first house in Scotland. We rented the bottom "flat." It was a fabulous house except for the bathroom and kitchen—afterthoughts to the house, added on for basic convenience.

I remember calling in a "joiner" (plumber) because there appeared to be a drip from the bathroom sink. He couldn't find anything wrong until he saw the small electric heater. "Why that there's your problem, luv! You've gone and got heat in here! Condensation! That's the problem. Now, get rid of that heater and you're set."

Burnbank, Auchamore Road, Dunoon, Scotland.

Our second house in Scotland. When Jim became CO of the Holland, we were given this wonderful house. The whole house was ours. Whereas "The Hollies" was on the water (Firth of Clyde), this was up in the hills by a burn (stream). Deer came into the garden and so did gnats. The air would be black with them.

I didn't want to move into this house. Julia had just been born and I didn't feel up to it. Jim said three words that convinced me—central heat, dryer.

6.
1978–81
Scotland

Scotland was just beautiful, so rugged, isolated . . . spiritual even. It never seemed real living there, more like a Disney movie set—sheep dogs rounding up sheep, hills purple with heather, woods so green and lush, compact villages of stone and white houses, and the most amazing rainbows.

I felt I was living in the nineteenth century with twentieth century expectations and obligations. Housing was hard to come by. Utilities were expensive—electricity so high only one room was heated in most homes, and there was a switch to heat the water. Our main source of heat was a coal fireplace. We were always cold. The only time I really got warm was when I was vacuuming.

Quilts were no protection against the cold here. Only wool blankets, sheep skin and down comforters. The milkman delivered milk in an open truck. The milk came in glass bottles, cream on top! Shopping was done daily in several shops. There was a shop that sold only baked goods, another for meat, another for vegetables, etc. Part of the town's social life. Great pace if all one had to do was the shopping and three o'clock tea.

I felt in a whirl. The social obligations overwhelmed me. Dinner parties, cocktail parties, light suppers, late suppers, luncheons, brunches, teas, coffees, club meetings and church socials. That's as close to crazy as I care to get. Of course, one word from me would have solved the problem . . . No!

I did enjoy one meeting, the Dunoon Needlework Guild. It grew out of quilting classes I had been teaching. Dunoon, as is most of the United Kingdom, was divided by class structure. Sewing crossed all social and economic barriers.

Cope. 1980.
Cotton, Satin, Linen.
Diane F. Wilson.

The rector at our church, Martin Shaw, had wanted a cope for ages. He asked me to make him one when he learned I sewed. His directions were simple when I asked him what a cope was. "It's a religious vestment. Should be easy . . . just a circle, I would expect, with a place cut out for my head."

The "Ladies Work Party" put up the money for the materials and I donated the labor. When Martin wore this in church, I felt so proud. Too proud, I think.

Julia was born. This time John and Rooie weren't as excited as they had been with James. Rooie groaned and John said, "You're not serious." They knew the work involved. Both, though, did pitch in with all that needed to be done to keep up with the house, yard, kids and entertaining.

Living in Scotland really taught me to appreciate the simple things in life. To get by on very little, to waste nothing, to value family time, to take motherhood seriously and calmly. It made me sad. I wanted to start over and do it right!

After three years and several months, it was time to leave. The *Holland* was to go to Charleston, South Carolina, to the shipyard. We were going back to Summerville!

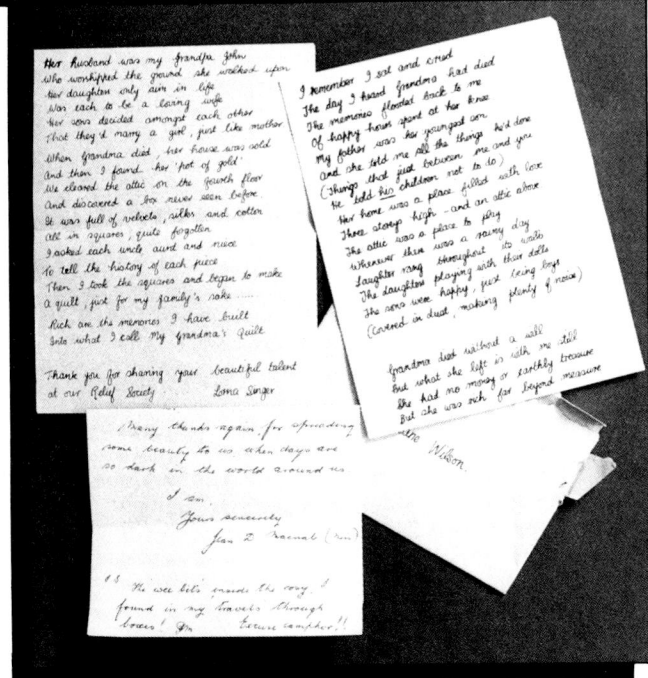

Holy Trinity Episcopal Church. Dunoon, Scotland.

The locals, almost all Presbyterian, called it "that English Church on the hill." The church was freezing cold! You had to know where to sit, only a few pews had heat.

Martin and his wife, Elsbeth, were wonderful people. They opened their home to everyone, and the whole congregation seemed happy to have a young family in the rectory.

Slowly though, Martin emptied the church of both Scots and Americans as he denounced the American Navy's presence in Dunoon as a threat to peace. That had to be one of the most painful experiences of my life. I wanted that cope back!

It has taken me a few years, but I wish Martin well and I understand his way of thinking.

Letter from WRI Group Poem.

I would be invited to speak to different groups on quilting. I always went. Church groups and the WRIs (Women's Rural Institute) mostly. Someone would always be appointed to give the "thanks." This poem and note are two examples.

49

Julia McCandless Wilson. 1981. Dunoon, Scotland.

My father's mother was named Beatrice McCandless, and her relatives were from Scotland, so Julia had a perfect middle name. The night she was born (February 20), the nurse who delivered the baby told me, "Sorry you're so cold in here, luv. Should have called ahead and we would have turned on the heat." That is true, and it was freezing cold.

Conditions in that hospital were basic, but more important, the staff treated every mom like a queen and acted like every baby was the best ever. Tea and toast were brought in between meals and the hard fast rule was everyone stayed a week! It was heaven.

Julia's Quilt. 1981. 30" × 22". Cotton. Diane F. Wilson.

Odd colors. Julia and I never liked it. She preferred an old flannel quilt James had.

50

Matthew's Quilt. *Carnation.* **1980.** Cotton. Diane F. Wilson.

My very good friend from Summerville was expecting a baby and I offered to do anything she wanted for this special baby. Tommie chose a Hawaiian baby quilt! The "baby" was four when I finished.

Dr. Lewis's magazine page.

Citadel Cadet. 1988. Charleston, South Carolina.

Citadel Cadet Quilt. 1980.
110" × 90". Cotton. Diane F. Wilson.

Before we left South Carolina my dentist, Dr. Lewis, a Citadel graduate had shown me a page in a magazine and asked me to make him a quilt like it. I said I would, bought fabric, batting and a special pen for marking the quilting pattern.

When I finished the quilt in Scotland and it was time to get rid of the "magic" marking lines, I had forgotten the combination. Cold water? Hot water? Hot iron? Cool iron? Nothing worked. I scrubbed with Tide and Ajax. Slowly, the bright blue lines faded, to soft blue lines. It made me sick.

52

Wilson children. 1981. Dunoon, Scotland. John, James, Jerusha, Julia.

The Holy Loch. Sandbank, Scotland.

The USS Holland, a submarine tender, is shown moored in the loch. Jim was Commanding Officer of this ship.
  We had climbed this hill, more like a mountain, to get this photo.

Mean Green. 1979.
90" × 65". Cotton.
Diane F. Wilson.

The nickname given to the local high school football team, "The Summerville Green Wave." While living in Scotland, the St. Paul's Episcopal Church Women asked me to make a raffle quilt for them as a fundraiser. I said I would and thought this idea would appeal to everyone. Apparently it did. The quilt was first prize on the raffle, over a moped and a microwave oven. That's true.

Sunshine and Flower. 1979.
Cotton. Diane F. Wilson.

If I told you that one year it rained or snowed 286 days, maybe more, you wouldn't believe it. It's true. I made this sunshine and hung it in my kitchen window.

The Scottish people all seemed to have green thumbs, for indoor or outdoor plants. Mine just turned yellow and mushy. So I made these.

The flowers were later published in Handmade *magazine.*

Meadowbrook Students and Me. 1985. Norfolk, Virginia.

I love all the children's faces. So full of hope. I think of a phrase used in church when babies are baptized—"You are the light of the world." Isn't that nice? I hate it that the light goes out for so many. Not at school, but at home.

7.
1981–85
South Carolina, Virginia

We were glad to be back in Summerville, at first. Everyone said how well we looked, hadn't changed at all. I thought, that's what being in a deep freeze for over three years will do.

Summerville didn't look good though. It just wasn't the same. Too many auto parts stores, every fast-food place you can imagine, stop lights at every intersection and so many new people that there were new Episcopal, Baptist and Methodist churches, and a new parish hall for the Lutherans. The town had turned into a city it seemed and ... Mrs. Westmoreland didn't know who we were. She would still call me over to the fence, only to ask if all those children were mine and to tell me about a special person who used to live in the house I was living in. Me. It broke my heart.

John left home. Went off to the Naval Academy. Oh, how we missed him. I never knew a good loss could feel so awful.

We were back in Summerville just long enough to get caught up on the house, the yard, get to the beach a few times and look for sharks' teeth in the Saw Mill Branch Canal.

Then, Jim got orders to Norfolk, Virginia.

How I hated that place! I don't even like the name. Jim decided we would live on base. I felt so trapped, so isolated, so identical. For excitement, James, Julia and I would look for lost balls on the golf course, and if really desperate, ride the elevator at the BOQ (Bachelor Officers' Quarters). Julia called it "riding the alligator."

There was a big grassy area between all the brick apartments with playground equipment, but no one ever seemed to be there. Then, because I was tired of sitting on the ground as I

57

watched my children swing, I wrote the CO of the base, asking for benches.

In no time at all, the benches were in place. And, out came all the moms, children, and sometimes, dads. At times, solutions to loneliness are simple.

Jim had been working long hours everyday. We hardly ever saw him. It seemed he was always gone whether he had shore or sea duty.

Then one night, he said the only things he cared about were his job, his car and jogging!

I could hear Ann Landers's voice. "Go get counseling."

Things improved, but not much. It was time to move again. The excitement of moving to a new place wasn't there. I felt tired!

James R. Wilson, Captain, United States Navy.

USS *Holland*, Charleston Harbor. 1982.

This blonde walked into the "O" Club lobby (there was a big party going on to welcome the ship and crew back), and went straight up to Jim.

"Hi ya, Captain."

"Who's that?" I asked.

"That," said Jim, smiling, "is my new navigator."

Looking for Sharks' Teeth. Saw Mill Branch Canal.

During certain months, when the snakes weren't out, it was great fun to look for sharks' teeth in the town's canal and creeks.

Town Talk

They asked him what his daddy did.

"Oh, let's see now, well he does a little huntin."

"Uh huh. That all?"

"Well, no. An a little fishin."

"Uh huh. What do you do?"

"Well, let's see now. Well. I hep my daddy."

"Well, I declare, she's a mess!"

"Stay sweet!"

"I hear, she drinks."

"He's got a girl friend down in Charleston. But his wife don't mind. You know how men are."

"Kids just running wild all over town and there she sits with her feet under the card table."

"Well, she was all done up, don't you know. Looked good, too, walking down the street. Wearing dead white folks clothes she said."

Candlewick Quilt. 1983. Corey Woods Garden Club. Summerville, South Carolina.
108" × 100". Cotton.

I won this quilt with a one dollar raffle ticket! I screamed when I heard the news. I don't recall winning anything so wonderful before. Some people in town said, "That's just what she needs! Another quilt."

I understood their feelings. But why not me? I have loved this quilt, appreciated it and so have others seeing it at shows and quilt lectures.

60

Grown Up Babies. Summerville. 1987.

When I went back for a visit, Eleanor got this picture of some of the babies, grown up now, with their quilts. They are from left to right: Megan Lomax, Joe Easely, Andrew Bense, Pamela and Sarah Bailey, Peter Bense and Robertson Griffith.

Priscilla Button with her granddaughter, Elizabeth, and daughter, Alden. Summerville. 1987.

I made a quilt for my friend Priscilla's first grandchild, just to celebrate the event. It made me feel old to have a friend who was a grandmother. Didn't bother Priscilla at all. Nothing does, I don't think. Could be wrong though.

Once when I admired her garden lettuce she said:

"I don't give my lettuce away.

People just want to put it under their tuna fish or something.

We eat our lettuce. Every bit."

Elizabeth is Priscilla's fourth or fifth grandchild; I lost track. Alden used to "fix-up" Rooie's hair and give John her old comic books when they were all much younger. I made Elizabeth a quilt for the memories.

Quilted Jacket. 1984.
Diane F. Wilson.

Perfect strangers have told me these colors are all wrong. I love the snaps.

Banner. 1985.
92" × 21". Cotton.
Diane F. Wilson.

This banner belongs to Meadow Brook Elementary School. I gave it to them for "staff appreciation" week. Teaching is one of the professions I admire most. Teachers need to get paid more money, for sure.

***Angel.* 1983.**
44" × 18". Cotton, Satin, Lace. Diane F. Wilson.

I call this angel an An-gel of the Lord now. Because of a conversation I had with Claire, then seven, after we moved to Alexandria, Virginia.

Claire and Julia had been asked to be in a Christmas play put on by two older girls, Girl Scouts, to earn a badge. Off they went full of enthusiasm only to return minutes later, furious and indignant.

"Mrs. Wilson! Do you know what that dumb ol' Allie did?

"Well, here she wanted us to be in her special ol' play and then she made me a goat and Julia a cow! And, I wanted to be an angel of the Lord!"

Claire

63

Eleanor's Quilt. 1984.

100" × 90". Cotton. Diane F. Wilson.

A simple design. Sometimes the simplest designs are best. I really like quilting a quilt. The rhythm is so relaxing. On the sketch I did for this quilt, Don, Eleanor's husband wrote this note to me—"8 lb 7 3/4 oz girl 6:32 AM March 22, 1983! All's well."

Quilted Bag. 1984.

34" × 20". Cotton. Diane F. Wilson.

I made this enormous bag because every time we went to the beach we had about nine plastic bags that said "Norfolk Naval Base." Julia could even fit into this when she wouldn't walk on the hot sand.

Album Quilt. 1985.
100" × 60". Cotton.
Diane F. Wilson.

I started this quilt in Summerville, getting fabric together for some squares to applique while waiting for housing in Scotland. When I made the squares I put in mostly things I missed in Summerville. Things left behind. Then, when I finally got around to the quilting, we were living in Norfolk and I was missing Scotland. So, the quilting pattern turned out to be thistles.

Album Quilt. 1985.
100" × 60". Cotton.
Diane F. Wilson.

Waiting to be quilted. I'm usually pretty good about finishing what I start, but this has been waiting for years now. That is James crawling around in that one square made in 1978.

65

James's and Julia's Bunk Bed Quilts. 1985.
70" × 46". Cotton. Diane F. Wilson.

We bought three sets of bunk beds for the town house in Alexandria. I hate bunk beds. I'm always bumping my head making them up or telling the kids "good-night."

I hurried with these quilts also. Instead of lumpy, they came out a bit cockeyed.

66

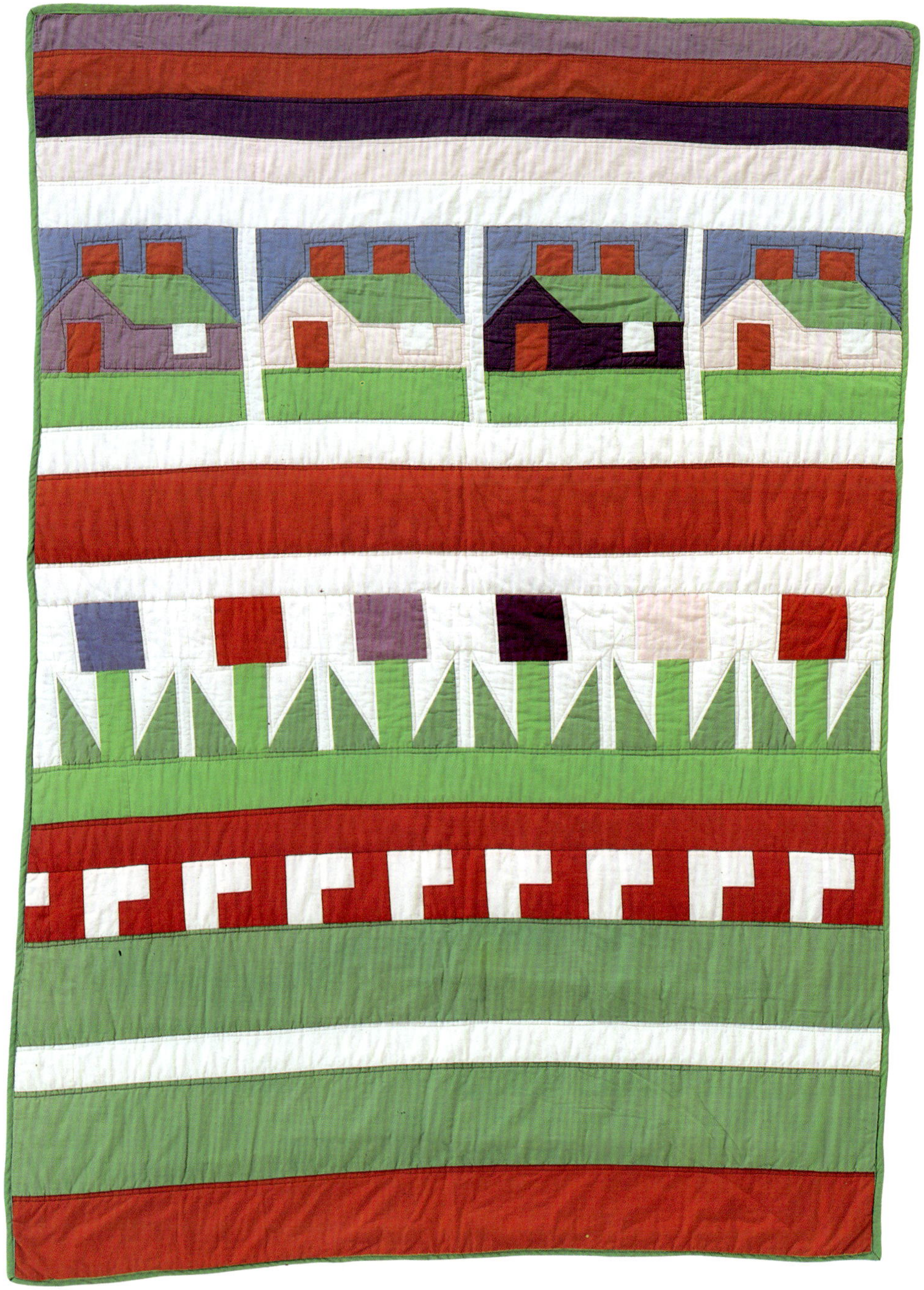

Wilson Family. 1986. Late Summer. Alexandria, Virginia.

This was the first time I ever had the family's photo taken for Christmas cards. Jim left that November. I used them anyway. I hate to be wasteful.

1985–
Virginia

We moved to Alexandria, Virginia into a townhouse one-half the size of any place we had ever lived before. Thank goodness we sold or gave away half of all our possessions before leaving Norfolk.

It felt sad, at first, to part with so much, but in the end, it felt free. The house, easy to clean, and the yard, easy to trim and weed, were compact. That felt free, too.

After a long time of being too busy to quilt as much as I would have liked, I was able to really get going again. I started selling items through shops, connected again with *McCalls*, and, thought about writing a book based on the quilt talks I gave to various groups.

The children were growing up . . . John graduated from the Naval Academy (one of the proudest days of my life!). Rooie started college at Virginia Tech, James went into fourth grade, Julia into first. For the first time in 22 years, I had everyone in school full time, or on their own. I really felt free now!

I waited for the empty feeling to hit me. It never did. At least not from the children leaving home or being in school. It came from where I least expected it, from Jim.

He left one Saturday. He took my identity (I thought), a TV and, except for one pathetic screwdriver in the drawer next to the stove, all the tools, moving into an apartment at the other end of town.

If people had told me that this was the best thing that could have ever happened to me, I would have slapped them. No one told me. But, it was.

Many nights I lay in bed wondering "why" and crying. As the tears rolled into my ears, I thought of a good country and western song—"I've got tears in my ears since yoooooou left!"

Naval Academy Graduates.

This is a family tradition—left to right . . . My father's father, my mother's father, Jim's father, my father, Jim, and our son John.

It occurred to me that I had half of my life left and it could be miserable or happy. Without really knowing how I would or could do, I chose to make mine happy.

Up until this time quilting had been a hobby. Now I took it seriously—got a tax number, business license, CPA, financial consultant, took business classes at T.C. Williams High School and started on a book that became an exhibition at The Athenaeum museum in Alexandria before the book got finished.

All this was positive action, but I felt we were just barely coping. Life was such a struggle, and I had such mixed feelings to deal with.

Then, the kids and I bought a kit to make a workbench. We read directions, hammered, screwed, drilled and finally there it was! It had a few mashed nails, a bottom shelf and blue letters across the back lip that said Hechingers (the local building suppliers). We were so proud of ourselves.

We went on to build a pegboard, then bought beautiful silver colored pliers and wrenches, a hammer and saw with wooden handles, screwdrivers, one with a lovely clear red handle and, finally, small containers filled with screws, nails, and tacks.

I knew then, we were going to be okay. We were going to make it.

Vest. *Home is Where the Heart Is.* **1986.**
Cotton.
Diane F. Wilson.

I thought about making cliche clothing . . .

Hey Mom

Over the years I have heard . . .

If I'd known this was a church camp, I wouldn't have come.

I didn't take it.

Now don't get excited but . . .

I didn't do it.

I hate it here.

Quick call the fire department! It's not my fault but the back yard is all on fire and . . .

Didn't you think those were good sentences? Would you take off for spelling?

Come see what the cat has by the back door. It's brown with . . .

You can't make me.

She made a face.

He started it!

That wasn't a burp.

You don't love me.

I promise. We'll be real quiet.

It won't make a mess.

Would you pick a dumb old drawing of a baseball field, not even drawn well, or a perfect drawing of a rocket?

You know I hate this food. You do this on purpose to make me mad.

It's sort of raining and, you know my hair, and these are good shoes and I need a ride to work. And, well, you're not doing anything.

He sat up front last time.

I'll do it later.

I was never allowed to do that.

When you come home, will you wake me up and kiss me?

Hearts and Flowers. 1986.

40" × 34". Cotton. Diane F. Wilson.

I was still in the soft color frame of mind. McCalls Needlework & Crafts *published this in their April, 1987 issue.*

The Company Sign. 1987.

My dad made this for me when I started my own business. I dream of seeing these letters on a huge building. We would have profit sharing, exercise time, child care, nutritious lunches and, I hope, great relations!

Sammy's Quilt. *Cats and Related Subjects*. 1986.
84" × 56". Cotton.
Diane F. Wilson.

We met Sammy and his sister, Agnes, because we saw and bought two of three "Low Country Scenes" Sammy had painted that were for sale at the Azalea Festival one year. Later, we went back to the shop, (next to Wesa's), and bought the other painting. That was how we started many years of friendship.

   Sammy has always loved cats. (Agnes hates them.) I decided it would be nice to make a cat quilt for Sammy as a present. (Sammy was always giving us his paintings and sketches.) I announced my plan to both Agnes and Sammy.

Sammy was thrilled and Agnes also. She liked for Sammy to be happy. Sisters are like that, I think. Well, Agnes never saw the quilt. She died of cancer. I felt awful. Sammy felt worse.

   I finished the quilt and really liked it. It felt so different from anything I had ever done. McCalls Needlework & Crafts liked it also, and published the quilt in their June, 1987 issue. I didn't want to give this quilt up.

   Sammy must have sensed this because when I wrote that I was sending it, he wrote he couldn't accept it—that it was "too much." We were stuck.

   I sent this quilt off to Sammy finally, dedicated to the memory of Agnes. (I can hear her now, "darn ol' cats!") It made us both feel better.

Sammy. 1987. Summerville, South Carolina.

Sammy's real name is Ravenal Gaillard. He loves cats and has more than this. People bring them to him and he won't say, "no." He pays the vet with money and original Low Country Scenes.

Baby and Children's Quilts

I never do the same thing twice. I can't say what makes me do one quilt one way, and then another quilt another way—a mood maybe. I do love these soft colors. Reminds me of spring and soft grasses and light flowers.

76

More Quilts for Children

I loved doing these quilts too. I think babies are more excited by bright colors than pale. Maybe not. Maybe it just makes them hyper.

It disappointed me, I have to admit, when McCall's Needlework & Craft *magazine didn't want to use these bright ones. It's hard not to take rejection personally.*

Christmas Quilt. 1988.

45" × 45". Cotton. Diane F. Wilson.

This quilt went to every soccer game last year. The sewing kept me from getting too serious, hollering too much. Some of the stitches are tight. Tension. It was a losing season.

Poster. 1988.

Pooka and I had gone to see the Georgia O'Keefe show in town and couldn't get in. So we went to see An American Sampler. *When I entered a room and saw this quilt, I couldn't believe my eyes! There was the quilt that had started it all for me!*

Quilted Jacket. *The Compulsive Woman.* **1988.**
Cotton. Cotton blends. Diane F. Wilson.

Sandra Simpson LeSound asked me to make her a compulsive woman jacket based on her book of the same name. I learned a lot from that book. And, I liked using sequins for the first time. Sandra's idea.

The compulsions are shown on the front only, the back and sides have to do with "recovery."

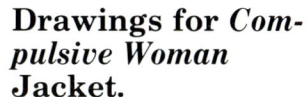

Drawings for *Compulsive Woman* Jacket.

79

Go Skins Sketch

Doug Williams foot was on the original drawing plan, but I cut the darn fabric too short (I told you earlier, I'm terrible at math). And so, I "made it work."

Go Skins. 1988.

80" × 60". Cotton. Diane F. Wilson.

I made this quilt for a raffle to benefit the interior restoration of Christ Church. The hardest part was getting Doug Williams's signature. At first I thought "MVP" had something to do with the Department of Motor Vehicles!

James helped with this quilt by giving me ideas and telling me the correct details.

Quilted Jacket. *Breaking Loose.* **1987.**
Cotton. Diane F. Wilson.

Angry and frustrated was how I was feeling when I started this. The colors reminded me of Amish quilts and I wondered then if those women ever got fed up and headed for city life? Or, electricity, at least.

Pillows. 1988.
Cotton. Diane F. Wilson.

McKitty "does" country.
  McKitty, observing the early bird.
  McKitty, all dressed up and no place to go.

Just for fun I made these, for a gallery. Later, it went out of business. I am starting to get a grasp on economics.

Peaches and Cream. 1987.
80" × 60". Cotton.
Diane F. Wilson.

James and Julia have a favorite story, Momotaro, Peach Boy, *which I read to them at least once a month. I was thinking of soft spring colors, and the idea of a quilt with peaches on it came to me, then cows, then a name, finally cream pitchers. It was fun. Someone told me that cows only see things upside down.*

And, this quilt reminds me of George Tupper, a dairy farmer from Summerville, South Carolina. He told me that the prettiest sight he ever saw was cows being herded into new grass, that they just kick up their heels. (Hoofs, he probably meant.)

McCalls Needlework and Crafts published this in June, 1989.

Katie's Quilts

Katie changed my life. I wrote her a note and told her so. I bet that embarrassed her.

I met Katie in a roundabout way. I was out looking for quilts to buy—a new business venture—and found out about her through a friend's cousin at a veggie stand on Route 236 in southern Maryland.

Katie is Amish, has seven daughters and one son, looks so frail, so serene. I want to tell her to "eat up."

In less than a year she has made seven quilts with help from her three oldest daughters. All beautiful, with tiny, perfect stitches. And, she stayed serene, with all in order—the children, the flower beds, the garden, the pots and pans, even the farm animals!

I had always experienced culture shock each time I saw Katie— now I felt something different. I felt threatened by her speed and ability, and I felt something really important was missing from my life although, God knows, it looked like we had it all. Anything and everything with a plug at the end of it!

I truly felt awash in chaos and confusion wondering how Katie could accomplish so much with so little. Then I began to see the answer.

Sloooowly, we have made some changes. It's never too late!

Epilogue

Jim did come back. But not until it was right for both of us. I learned I could only change myself, to detach, to live one day at a time.

We're moving again. In summer, after school is out. Back to Summerville! Town has changed even more. There are two Summerville zip codes now. The Piggly Wiggly moved out to Oakbrook Plaza . . . and the train that used to stop for freight now just heads up to Ridgeville. Mrs. Westmoreland died. Annie and Zeb, too, also Dr. Lewis, Shirley Cates and the disapproving Mrs. Rawls who lived behind us.

Jim is retiring from the Navy. He's not sure what he's going to do down there. But, I know what I want to do—open a quilt shop, design and make quilts, write a "how to" book. And, of course, go to Edisto, hunt for sharks' teeth in the canals, and sit on my front porch, sewing and listening for the train coming up from Lincolnville.

206 E. Richardson Avenue.

Our house in Summerville. Jim wants to put "modern" windows in because the weights and ropes that make the windows go up and down are always breaking. I hate to see the ripply glass panes go. I'm not for progress.

**Diane F. Wilson.
Alexandria, Virginia.
1989.**

People can't believe what I look like now compared to my wedding picture. I'm afraid to ask why.

Thoughts

If you were to ask me, I would say use your quilts. However, quilts don't like to go to the beach, on picnics or to be used for moving furniture. Quilts worn to a certain softness feel so good—like bannisters and stairs. The touch of all of them makes me feel connected to others.

I do love making quilts. It's a way of life for me. Business and pleasure. Things are right with the world when I'm quilting.

Making quilts is something anybody can do, if they want. It's like cooking—you can get fancy with roasts, or keep it simple and fry hamburger. It's all the same. Everybody eats. You just have to believe in yourself. That's the hardest part. Of anything.